THE MIDDLE GROUND

CASUAL ELEGANCE FOR THE MODERN MAN

Easy and Elegant Life, LLC

The Middle Ground© 2019 T. Christopher Cox.
All rights reserved under the International and Pan-American Copyright Conventions. No part of this book may be reproduced or transmitted in any form or by any means, electronic or mechanical, including photocopying, recording, or by any information storage and retrieval system, without permission in writing from the publisher.

Warning: the unauthorized reproduction or distribution of this copyrighted work is illegal. Criminal copyright infringement, including infringement without monetary gain, is investigated by the FBI and is punishable by up to 5 years in prison and a fine of $250,000.

The Middle Ground, Always Presentable.

When I was just turning thirteen, my father retired from a lifetime of service as a U.S. Army Officer. Until the day he retired his weekday sartorial choices had been limited to the "uniform of the day." Weekends were fairly easy to pull off in Europe and back home in suburban America, but when he was faced with what to wear, "day-to-day," out in the world, he was a bit up in the air.

Until he found <u>Dress for Success</u> by John T. Molloy, his copy of which sits on my bookshelf to this day. Dad took that book to heart and became one of the best dressed men I had encountered.

Naturally, I tore through his copy to see how I, as an aspiring dater, could improve my image. When my parents enrolled me in prep school, I took my new-found knowledge and turned to my father's clothier, Mark Wilson, then of Britches of Georgetowne. (Mark if you're out there, thank you!) Blue blazer, dress khakis, check. Brooks Brothers button-down shirts and penny loafers? check. Lacoste polo shirts? Yup.

And so it began.

I eventually joined up for a couple of years— Britches, not the military — and fought the good fight to help men dress better. Then I got sidetracked with a career in advertising, never losing touch with the periodicals, books, and any other media I could find, relating to menswear. I became deeply interested in the bespoke process, I celebrated the return to elegance that birthed *The Rake* magazine. I started working with my custom tailor to design my own garments.

And somewhere in there, around the turn of the century, I started a blog.

EasyandElegantLife.com was founded with the intention of bringing some sartorial know-how and a blueprint for living well to those who were just starting out in life. Since then the internet has exploded with advice for the younger set.

These days, I get most of my questions from my clients and readers who are middle-aged or older. They are confused about how to dress well when they aren't boardroom ready or set to work in the yard.

There has to be more to the spectrum than dark jeans, chinos, checked button-downs and polo shirts.

With more choices than ever before, dressing well, all the time, should be easy, but often becomes confusing for the man used to the old rules. To be sure, google "elegant men" and you'll get a lot of photos of well (if too tightly)-tailored, suited and booted (younger) men. Guys in casually elegant and appropriate clothing are rarely to be seen.

So what is a modern man of a certain age to do? Where can we turn for inspiration?

I hope that you will turn to the lessons I present in this booklet. Here you will find some simple ideas for remaining stylish while ignoring the extremes of fashion during these increasingly casual days.

Getting Started

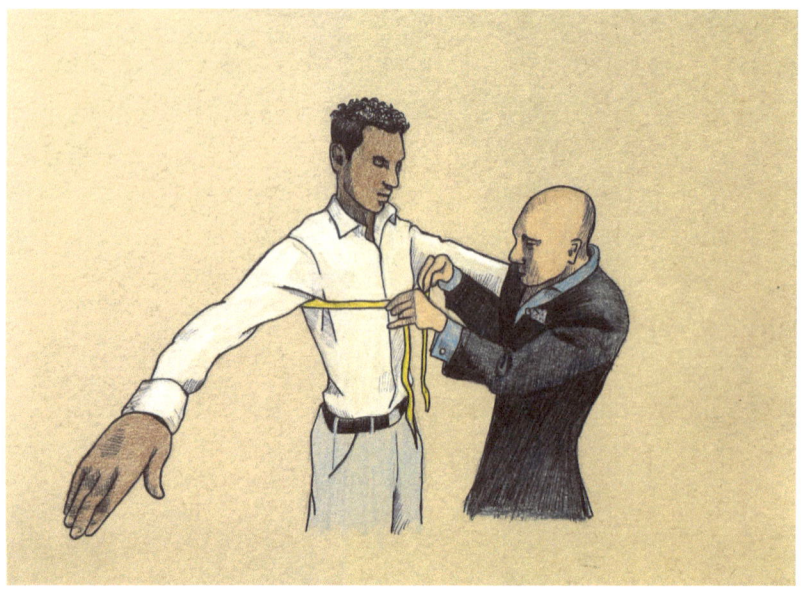

Time to edit your closet. If your clothing is too out-of-date, too baggy, ill-fitting, boxy, or worn out, get rid of it. You've made it to a certain point in your life, make sure that you look like it.

Your clothing should be tailored to your shape. It doesn't have to be skinny, or tight, just well-tailored. That may mean shirts and blazers with slightly higher armholes, and less room around the middle. Your blazers and jackets should have a bit of waist suppression, and be long enough to cover the seat of your trousers. The shoulders should fit yours, not hang over so much that they droop. The coat should button around your natural waist. Armholes (scyes) are higher, yes, you'll feel them, but they will actually give you more freedom of movement. It sounds counter-intuitive, but for proof, look to Fred Astaire dancing. His (and your) coat won't ride up as much if it fits at the collar, shoulder, and armhole.

Trousers shouldn't flap in the wind, a trimmer silhouette will suit just about everyone. Trim doesn't mean "skinny," I can't emphasize that enough. Aim for trousers that are comfortable around the seat and thigh, but taper to just touch the top of your shoe.

Shoes are another potential pitfall. Too often I see men wearing awful looking shoes. I get it, they are extremely comfortable. As a former dance instructor and fencer, I understand foot pain. But, investing in some good insoles and wearing them inside of decent, polished, leather shoes with a slightly rounded or almond--shaped toe will do wonders in elevating your overall stylishness. That means resisting the siren's call of square toes, trail/hiking shoes, running shoes, and other shapeless styles.

By limiting your palette, your clothes will mix and match nicely. "Color is tricky after a certain age," cautions my friend The Architect. "Too loud and you look like you've won the PGA." But, that doesn't mean you have to stick to drab and safe. If you like to add color, great! Choose accent pieces and accent sparingly.

There you have the bones of the thing. Let's start to flesh things out.

Chapter 1
THE SLIDING SCALE OF FORMALITY

The Sport Coat and Blazer

There are those who will tell you that today you can go just about anywhere with a sport coat or blue blazer. I'm one of them.

Short of an invitation to a black tie event, you can get away with wearing a blue blazer just about everyday and in almost all situations. A well cut blazer matches any trouser, including jeans, that you care to pair it with. Always pack a blue blazer. My suggestion is to ignore the brass/metallic button route and opt instead for brown or navy horn, which makes the blazer easier to wear everywhere. Have one for warmer months and one for colder. In chilly climates, you may consider a double-breasted version. Today's cuts are far less boxy than those of the preceding decades. With the DB, you may want to wear brass buttons harkening back to the blazer's naval heritage. The trimmer cut on the new models also means that you can wear them unbuttoned to give you an even more casual air. But should the occasion call, you are ready to be buttoned up and always presentable.

Although a sport coat is less formal than the blazer, it can still be considered a workhorse of your Middle Ground wardrobe. In winter, a tweed of any color, and in summer a lighter palette with a pattern, will both serve you well. I tend to stick to earthy colors or a light blue with a pattern of tans and grays that will go well with light gray trousers and khakis. The earthy colors pair nicely with cream and khaki, and yes, gray. Particularly if the buttons are light brown horn or creamy tan/off-white.

The Sweater

A staple in any casually elegant wardrobe is the sweater. Worn with, or without a blazer or sportcoat, it can give a more finished look to your casually elegant appearance.

Warmer months will call for a linen/cotton mix, silk, or a fine-gauge cashmere. All are very useful when we go from outside temperatures to climate controlled interiors. I recommend a crew neck and a cardigan. Both styles set off a dress shirt in different ways.

The crew neck eliminates the need for a tie, and the cardigan works equally well with or without neckwear.

Winter is always sweater weather! A chunky cardigan and a crew neck, and heavier gauge cashmere will be worth the up front cost in daily use. In addition, I really like the button up funnel neck sweater, a cashmere polo collar, and a merino turtleneck (roll neck) to wear with tailored trousers when you don't feel like reaching for a dress shirt.

The idea is to look like you've put some thought into your appearance rather than simply having forgotten your tie. That's not to say that each of these styles isn't going to work with a dress shirt layered underneath.

Even a turtleneck can work well under a shirt for a sort of '70s vibe, or the shirt can be worn collar up and peeking out under the roll neck in the casually sophisticated Italian style.

A sweater is a deliberate statement of smart casual.

Chapter 2
SPEAKING OF SHIRTS

THERE ARE NO SHORT SLEEVED DRESS SHIRTS.

The key to shirts that suit the middle ground of dressing well is the shirt collar. It must be firm enough to stand up on its own, without the aid of a tie, under a coat collar. For this reason I prefer to have my shirts custom made with higher collar bands and sometimes with hidden button-down collars (as seen in the illustration.)

Because of the absence of a tie, many men will elect to punch up the color and pattern of their shirts — relying on spots, loud stripes, dark backgrounds, or checks to enliven an outfit. I'm not one of them. I like the look of stripes and checks, but see them used so often that they risk being the "default" choice. I think it is more elegant to use texture in the fabric to subtly enhance the overall look. Choices in textured shirtings may include: dobbys; poplins, twills, herringbones; satin stripes; pinpoints; brushed cotton; flannel; and, linens. Pale blue and white are the two most useful colors, followed by lavender, and pink. Bonus points if you find the right shade of ivory for your complexion.

All that is not to say that you should steer clear of stripes and checks! I prefer mixing two colors for the most part: tan and blue, green and blue, or blue and white. Lighter gray is also very useful. Rarely are the stripes I wear thicker or bolder than pencil stripes, but don't let that stop you from experimenting. Just remember the rule that the patterns that lie next to each other should be of differing scales to avoid making the observer's eyes spin.

The polo shirt is the choice for casual Friday offices, and they are great to wear during the warmer months. As with your button-up shirts, you might opt for the smoother textures over the ubiquitous piqué cotton (especially if they aren't box-fresh.)

The ability to stand up under a sport coat is also to be considered. Polo shirt collars don't do this and will either have to be buttoned all the way up, or spread over the collar of the coat. They also require ironing to make sure the points don't start to curl up.

Wearing your polo collar over the collar of your sports coat works best with more casual suits and sport coats of cotton or linen. Otherwise, wear your polos with tailored trousers. There is a brand called Eidos which makes a "dressier" long-sleeved polo shirt called the Lupo. Its collar is taller and made to be worn with coats and jackets. Mack Weldon and Sunspel do a micro-mesh short sleeve that allows every breeze to pass through. The collar lays nicely, too. Both are well worth a look. It goes without saying that the polo shirt will be worn tucked in unless the day calls for very relaxed clothing and the bottom of the shirt is square cut rather than shaped like a dress shirt's tails.

Chapter 3
WAIST DOWN

FINISH THE MASTERPIECE

We've learned a bit about your top half, now it is time to complete the picture. It's not just at the gym, that I see men who nail the upper body and totally ignore their lower halves.

KEEP YOUR PANTS ON (POINT) — TROUSERS

"Is that where you normally wear your pants?"
My tailor Larry Wood will ask.

The gentleman will then hike them up to his natural waist. Which isn't where they will end up, barring the use of braces/suspenders, which have fallen out of favor in the last decades. So Larry will make sure that the trousers are cut appropriately, to sit as well as possible if they fall below a belly, or onto the hips. That's the advantage of custom and bespoke tailoring. If you're buying off the rack, you can't be assured that the trouser has been cut to fit you. This is where your expert alterations tailor comes in handy.

The key to trousers (as in jeans) is fit. With a correctly fitted trouser, a man may wear any style elegantly, from single- and double-pleated, forward or reverse, to flat-front.

It is my opinion that the trouser looks best when worn in the Italian fashion, that is long enough to just rest on the top of the shoe. I used to wear a full break on fuller trousers. I looked like I borrowed my father's suit.

Today, I prefer a trouser that tapers and is closer cut at the calf with substantial cuffs (turn-ups) at the bottom whose weight keeps the trouser leg resting on the top of the shoe without flapping about when I walk. When you are wearing a suit or sport coat, this is the part of the trouser that is most on display, so you may as well show off the shoe and get it right.

Braces, Belts, and Side Adjusters.

Where your trousers sit is a matter of personal preference. A lot of fashion has shown the trouser riding on the hips as if they were a pair of jeans. That's because most young people, at whom fashion is targeted, have grown up wearing jeans and are used to the fit. That's fine. If that's where you like them, have at it.

In the past, men grew up wearing trousers with a higher rise. They are more comfortable, allow for pleats, and cover the stomach. They also require a great fit to stay in place unless they are worn with suspenders/braces. That's fine, too. They look best with an extended tab closure at the front and cuffs/turn-ups to help them fall correctly.

Suspenders, or braces, are really the best option as far as comfort and keeping your trousers seated at your natural waist. Each strap is also able to be adjusted to accommodate dropped shoulders.

When trousers are made to be worn with braces, they are higher rise, frequently have a fish-tail back and are cut with an inch to spare around the waist. Braces also ensure that pleats will fall correctly to the cuff/turn up at the ankle which adds weight to help keep the creases in line.

Belts are almost the default for most men. This is because almost all off the rack trousers are designed with belt loops. If you choose to wear a belt, make it a very good belt.

What constitutes a very good belt? Construction and materials. The best belts are either solid leather or two strips of leather bonded and sewn around a lining material.

Belt leathers should match your shoes in terms of color and texture. So a suede shoe calls for a suede belt in the same color (or very close.) Cordovan matches cordovan, etc…

The only exception I make is to wear alligator straps without having invested in alligator shoes. Exotic skin belts go with everything as far as I'm concerned. Just match the color and the belt buckle to your shoes and other metals that you wear (watch bands or bevels, wedding ring, etc…)

Somewhere in the middle falls the side adjuster at the waistband of the trousers. These are buckles and straps or buttons that allow for the fit to be taken in or let out whenever necessary. Thanksgiving dinner, for instance. This style also looks best with an extended tab closure, and is very convenient when worn through TSA checkpoints.

PUTTING YOUR FOOT IN IT: CHOOSING YOUR SHOES

I see plenty of decently dressed men around town, until you take in the whole picture and get to their choices of shoe. I say shoe, because there is one style that seems to have taken my town by storm — the driving moc — for better and all too often for worse. I'll explain why later.

There are a number of shoe styles that are appropriate for The Middle Ground dresser. Some for business, others that are best left to creatives and freelance types or for evenings out, and those that do double duty. Here are my recommendations.

The Loafer

The king of Middle Ground shoes has to be the loafer in its many forms. A loafer is any laceless, slip-on shoe. Loafers range from the more formal to the most casual.

The Tassel Loafer

Just what is sounds like — a loafer with a pair of tassels at the tongue. This one is near the top of the formal loafer scale. It can be worn with a suit. The genius of the tassel loafer is that it goes equally well with blazers/sport coats, khakis, jeans, cords and wool trousers. It is so versatile a shoe that I recommend buying at least two pair, one in black with minimal decoration, and one in brown — either suede or calf skin.

The Penny Loafer

Penny loafers come in two varieties — full strap and half strap. That is to say a shoe with the strap that goes down to the instep and one that stops just over the top of the moccasin apron. Fulls straps are a bit dressier, in my opinion. I also think that those which feature a "beef role" (the heavy welt across the back at the heel) are too informal for pairing with anything other than jeans or khakis. The traditional oxblood color is very versatile, as is a tan or dark brown. Lots of men wear black Penny Loafers with khakis. I have never been able to make that work (perhaps if I were in the armed services where black shoes are the rule.) Suede versions are always interesting to the eye and can be worn year-round.

The Belgian Loafer

I love 'em. The Belgian shoe is a design that has been around for eons and was handmade in Belgium. The design has a pointed tongue, an apron welt around the front, a low-to-non-existent heel, and a string bow as ornamentation. Many can't stand them, thinking they're too effete with that little string bow. They are also horrible for those of us with flat feet, offering no support at all. But, they are the closest things to slippers that you can wear and they go with everything from jeans to tuxedos. They may be the perfect shoe to fly in, too. The very louche, soft-soled "Mr. Casual" offered by Belgian Shoes, in New York, is ridiculously comfortable. Other versions can be had with hard leather soles, but what's the point?

LACE-UPS

Those of you who must wear lace up shoes rejoice! There are a lot of options out there that work very well with The Middle Ground wardrobe.

THE DERBY

A derby, or blucher, is a style that has an open lacing system. That is, there are two pieces of leather sewn on top of the vamp and tongue through which the shoe laces pass. They fit almost everyone very well. They are considered less formal than the oxford with its closed laces. I like derbies without decoration and that aren't too clunky looking. In black they are great city shoes, in brown scotchgrain (leather with a pebbly texture, sort of like an American football) with a lug sole, they make a wonderful choice for the rain.

THE CHUKKA

The chukka, aka the desert boot, is a short boot that laces up. Originally made in unlined suede, it is a style that works in calfskin and shell cordovan, too. The key to making this work with The Middle Ground, is to choose a pair with a hard leather sole, a chiselled or almond-shaped toe, and only two eyelets for laces. It makes them sleeker. Dark brown or Polo suede looks especially well with jeans, cords and gray trousers.

THE CHELSEA

Otherwise known as The Beatle Boot after being adopted by the fab four. The Chelsea boot is a workhorse. In black, polished up, it can be worn with suits or tuxedos, blazers and gray flannels. In brown calf or brown suede it works as nicely with jeans as with cords, khakis, and gray flannels, if they are slim cut. The slimmer opening at the ankle is kind to the boot, and a shaped toe (again, chiselled or almond-shaped) gives it a more formal look that will never be confused with your Timberlands.

Other Styles of Shoes

The Boat Shoe

If there is one shoe that is ubiquitous on the East Coast of the United States, it's the boat shoe or camp moc. There's a reason for their popularity, they are comfortable and pretty much indestructible. They're made to get wet, after all. I love a good LL Bean bison camp moc and wear them frequently with jeans, khakis, shorts or bathing trunks. I limit their appearances to doing house things, trips to the hardware store or boat rides when it's too cold to go barefoot. They are far too casual to fall into The Middle Ground of dressing. Italians, however, manage to get away with them in coloured suede versions, but I would suggest wearing them in very casual settings only.

The Monk Strap

Stylish, unusual, and falling somewhere in formality between the loafer and the blucher, the monk strap (either double or single), with its buckle(s) is an interesting shoe. Suits to jeans, the monk strap is at home in The Middle Ground. Italians will wear double monks with one strap unbuckled in a show of *sprezzatura*. Know your audience before trying to pull off this sort of eccentricity. Toe-capped, brogued, and pain toe version are all available and reflect the wearer's individual tastes. I prefer mine in plain toe or cap-toe styles. Read into that what you will. A classic Middle Ground configuration might be the brown suede, double-monk with a cap-toe, or the tan calf, single-monk with a chiselled toe.

The Driving Moc

I have a love/hate relationship with my driving mocs. At one time I wore them so often that they became slippers when the rubber studs on the bottom wore out. They look great with slim cut jeans and khakis. They don't do well at all with fuller cut trousers that tend to puddle around the ankles with such a low cut shoe. I really don't like the drivers with the full rubber sole that wraps to the heel. They just look clunky to my eye. Choose the version most true to the original racing shoe and opt for the pebbled/cleated sole.

The Velvet Slipper

The dandies among us will wear velvet slippers (either embroidered with metallic thread or not) with jeans, shorts, and evening clothes. I think they belong best at home. In a business setting, people will spend far too much time looking at your shoes rather than hearing what it is that you have to say. That said, they are an excellent shoe to wear with a dinner jacket, or with jeans and a black roll(turtle) neck and black blazer for a casual evening out.

Chapter 4
DETAIL ORIENTED

ACCESSORIES MATTER

Now that the masses have begun to crow about the death of the tie (whose demise is greatly exaggerated) many a man might wonder how to express a bit of personality in how he presents himself.

Neckwear

In certain circles the necktie is still a powerful symbol. The good news is that there really are only a few ties you need to keep in your wardrobe to be ready for just about anything.

To go with anything blue, choose a solid navy grenadine or silk knit tie. Compliment this with a small patterned blue tie - maybe in small dots, or stripes.

A silver patterned tie, a glen check or Prince of Wales (the glen check with an overplaid), is useful for more formal evening situations where you might wear your navy blazer and gray trousers with a white shirt and black shoes.

A black tie in grenadine or silk knit takes you through a funereal and goes well with any gray patterned sports coats.

That's really about it. I like to buy ties that are 8 mm - 9 mm wide at most as they never go in or out of fashion and work with all kinds of tailoring. You may indulge in bowties, or ties in your school colors or regimental stripes, armed services stripes and the like if you've served.

Scarves, on the other hand, are something which I think you can't have enough of. Cashmere scarves keep you warm. Silk scarves or silk and wool, or silk and linen scarves work when cashmere is too warm. Cotton or linen scarves are great for the heat when you may have to dab your forehead or not perspire into your shirt collar. Anything from a shawl sized pashmina to a desert conquering shemagh, to a neckerchief sized tengui or bandana is going to come in handy for something, sometime.

Spectacles, wallet, and watch

Eyeglasses are rife with opportunity to express yourself. I tend to wear rounded frames in tortoise. If they're readers, have some fun. For sunglasses, Ray Ban Wayfarers or Aviators will always be stylish and look great on just about everybody.

A quick word about your wallet. If it's bulging, it's time to trade it in and switch to a cardholder. Cash, in that case, is held by a money clip in a different pocket. If you must carry a larger wallet, consider a breast pocket model and keep it the inside pocket of your blazer or sport coat.

Your watch, like your shoes, speaks volumes about your style. I prefer the classics that aren't too big or flashy. A stainless steel Rolex, a Cartier or Hamilton rectangular tank with a gold rim and alligator strap, your father's or grandfather's watch, or a simple Seiko dive watch are all easy to find and wear with just about anything. Leather straps should match your belt and shoes. Metals should echo other metals like your belt buckle, monk straps, glasses, etc...

Pocket Litter

Pocket dumps are very fashionable among the EDC community and are one of my favorite features in "The Rake" magazine. I'm always interested in the things we carry on our persons. There are a few things I find invaluable.

A good pocket knife. From a Swiss Army Knife, to a classic slip joint like a small Case knife you will always find a use for a small blade. Even if it's just to open envelopes.

A small notebook is invaluable for jotting down brilliant ideas, contact information, good quotations, book suggestions and the like.

As long as you're taking notes, why not do so with a good pen. President Kennedy carried a Parker Jotter. The Space Pen by Fisher writes in any condition, upside down and underwater. Fountain pens are works of art, a delight to use, and collect. They don't have to be the most expensive, either! I have a number of vintage daily writers and use a $20 Pilot Metropolitan, too.

Finally, let's talk about keys. I try not to carry more than two to three keys at one time. My two house keys are kept in a leather sleeve made by Bellroy; my car key is kept by itself, often in a different pocket, or in a briefcase or shoulder bag.

Jewelry

I'm old-school about jewelry. I believe that your watch counts, as does a signet or wedding ring. That's about all I think you should sport. If necklaces, and bracelets are your thing, great! Just remember your audience and choose accordingly.

The Manbag

Which bag should you carry? A tote? Briefcase? Leather envelope? Shoulder bag? Backpack?

Yes. Whichever suits your style and needs. You're going to have to have somewhere to keep receipts and business cards now that you've gotten rid of that overstuffed wallet. And we all have laptops, phones, and tablets that need housing. Just make sure that you don't hang the strap over your shoulder when you are wearing your sport coat or blazer. It skews the jacket and looks awful. You want to have some way of carrying it either tucked under an arm or by the handle.

Hats

Hats can be tricky. They are very useful, but can be hard to pull off for many men. I find the pub hat or newsboy cap a good option for winter (or in linen, for summer.) If you choose to wear a ball cap, please consider finding one in an unexpected fabric and without a logo. Fedoras, trilbys, and porkpies are all wonderful in fur, felt or straw. But put some wear on them. All hats look best after they've taken on some personality with use.

Outerwear

You only need three styles of outerwear garments to cover your needs. My general rule of thumb is that the jacket or coat should be long enough to cover your blazer.

The warm topcoat

Either double-breasted or single with raglan sleeves, the topcoat is more than heavy enough in today's climate controlled life to take on winter. I find that a classic camel hair is a stylish choice, but black or navy cashmere is very elegant and will serve you as well.

The waterproof layer

A classic like the trench coat is the obvious choice, but the single breasted "Mac" will always be in style. Typically I wear a khaki version, but I also have a white trench coat that I will wear year-round. If you're more the outdoorsy type, you might want to invest in a waxed cotton coat, like the Barbour. The Beaufort is the version that is long enough to cover your sport coat and looks great as part of that sports wear/tailored clothing mix.

Honorable mention to anything with a hood if you don't like wearing hats or carrying an umbrella. Lots of labels are now making car coats with hidden hoods that would be a very good choice for those who like to travel light.

The lightweight jacket

When spring and fall temperatures make wearing anything too heavy too hot, the lightweight jacket is the answer, particularly if you are not going to be wearing a blazer or sport coat (topped off with a scarf, they will be warm enough to serve as light weight top layers.)

In recent years, the safari jacket (also seen in styles like the M65 field jacket, or Norfolk style jacket) has made a comeback. I find these coats to be really useful with their multiple pockets, throat closures, rollable sleeves and belts that add shape. Some are even water resistant. Long enough to cover a sport coat, and comfortable enough to cover a light sweater or polo shirt, the safari jacket is a workhorse and stylish to boot. If it's in the budget, La Stoffà makes a custom version in lightweight suede, linen/cotton, or leather.

Chapter 5
GETTING IT TOGETHER

We've been wearing business casual for decades now, but most of us just can't seem to get it right, or care to even try. Since you're reading this, I know that you're one of the few who actually cares how he looks and wishes to put his best foot forward in all situations.

In the previous chapters I've outlined some basics to get you started, but I would be remiss if I didn't point out a very important fact; to show you to your best advantage, your clothing must relate to your appearance. In other words, to both your skin/hair color and your physical shape.

Everything doesn't work on everyone.
Yes, models can wear almost anything, but put the wrong colors next to their faces and even the most attractive will look sallow and sickly.

So, if you're skinny, don't wear really baggy clothing. If you're more stout, don't pour yourself into a wetsuit-looking-skinny-fit *anything*. Have your tailor fit you accordingly. and remember: proportion and color matter.

Finally a word about fit. How wide, how short, how … whatever? I hear it over and over. Here are my rules of thumb. Have the sleeves of your jacket shortened to your wristbone. Your shirt cuffs should reach to the base of your palms. You should see about a 1/8" - 1/4" of shirt cuff below your jacket sleeve. The shoulders of your jacket shouldn't droop because they are too wide for you. The cuffs or hems of your trousers should just rest on the tops of your shoes (and that means when your wear your trousers at whatever spot above, below or at your actual waist you really wear your trousers.) There should be no bunching, pulling, stretching, opening or gaping around pockets, pleats, vents, waists, lapels, and collars. That's it. Find a great alterations tailor and treat him like gold.

Congratulations, you've made it this far and I bet you grasp the concept: don't just choose "default," do a little more than you have to and be amazed at how much better you'll look and feel.

About The Author

Christopher Cox is a blogger, content creator, copywriter and men's wardrobe consultant. Inspired by the biography <u>Everybody Was So Young</u> by Amanda Vaill, he began EasyAndElegantLife.com where he explores the art of living well. He is a two-time cancer survivor, happily married to an extraordinary woman, and proud father to a daughter, a son, and two Jack Russell terriers.

Dalyn Montgomery is a writer and illustrator whose body of work attempts to incorporate diverse interests and experiences into one aesthetic whole. He is the sole contributor at www.brohammas.com.

www.ingramcontent.com/pod-product-compliance
Lightning Source LLC
Chambersburg PA
CBHW041819040426
42452CB00004B/153